Published in 2013 by The Rosen Publishing Group, Inc.
29 East 21st Street, New York, NY 10010

Photo Credits: **KEY** t=top; l=left; r=right; tl=top left; tcl=top center left; tc=top center; tcr=top center right; tr=top right; cl=center left; c=center; cr=center right; b=bottom; bl=bottom left; bcl=bottom center left; bc=bottom center; bcr=bottom center right; br=bottom right; bg=background

CBT = Corbis; GI = Getty Images; iS = istockphoto.com; TF = Topfoto; TPL = photolibrary.com; wiki Wikipedia

7tr CBT; **8**cl iS; bl TF; **10**c, cr TF; **10–11**tc wiki; **11**cr, tr TF; **12–13**tc TF; **14–15**bg CBT; **15**cr iS; tl wik **16**br iS; tc TF; **17**bc, bl, br, tc, tl, tr iS; **18**bc, cr GI; bl iS; **19**bg GI; **20**bl TF; **20–21**bc TPL; **21**cr TF; **22–23**bc TF; **26**bc SH; br TF; **26–27**bg CBT; **27**bc SH; br TF; **28**bl GI; **29**bg TF

All illustrations copyright Weldon Owen Pty Ltd. **front cover**, **1**c, **6**b, **12**b, **14–15**, **16–17**, **18**tr, **21**tl, **22–23**, **24–25**, **30–31** Malcolm Godwin/Moonrunner Design

Weldon Owen Pty Ltd
Managing Director: Kay Scarlett
Creative Director: Sue Burk
Publisher: Helen Bateman
Senior Vice President, International Sales: Stuart Laurence
Vice President Sales North America: Ellen Towell
Administration Manager, International Sales: Kristine Ravn

Library of Congress Cataloging-in-Publication Data

Park, Louise, 1961–
 Blood in the arena : gladiators of ancient Rome / by Louise Park.
    p. cm. — (Discovery education: ancient civilizations)
 Includes index.
 ISBN 978-1-4777-0054-9 (library binding) — ISBN 978-1-4777-0093-8 (pbk.) —
 ISBN 978-1-4777-0094-5 (6-pack)
 1. Gladiators—Juvenile literature. I. Title.
 GV35.P368 2013
 796.80937—dc23
                          2012019579

Manufactured in the United States of America

CPSIA Compliance Information: Batch # W13PK2: For Further Information contact Rosen Publishing, New York, New York at 1-800-237-9932

ANCIENT CIVILIZATIONS

BLOOD IN THE ARENA
GLADIATORS OF ANCIENT ROME

LOUISE PARK

PowerKiDS press

New York

Contents

The Roman Gladiators

Gladiators were trained fighters who performed for crowds throughout the Roman Empire. They fought each other and even wild animals. Sometimes they fought to the death, using weapons such as swords and spears. The Roman Empire was one of the most powerful empires in history. It began around 27 BC and lasted until about AD 395. The gladiators started performing even before the Empire began, with gladiatorial training generally used as a form of punishment for slaves, prisoners of war, and criminals. Rome's first gladiatorial games took place in 264 BC. They began a tradition of fighting for entertainment that continued for more than 660 years.

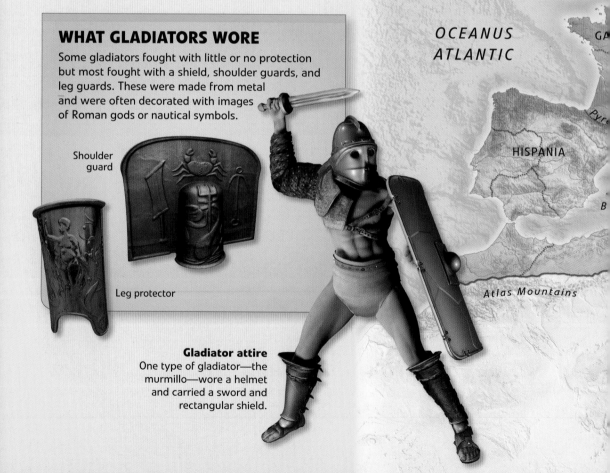

WHAT GLADIATORS WORE

Some gladiators fought with little or no protection but most fought with a shield, shoulder guards, and leg guards. These were made from metal and were often decorated with images of Roman gods or nautical symbols.

Shoulder guard

Leg protector

OCEANUS
ATLANTIC

BRI

GA

HISPANIA

B

Pyr

Atlas Mountains

Gladiator attire
One type of gladiator—the murmillo—wore a helmet and carried a sword and rectangular shield.

Scenes in stone

The Romans used mosaics made from tiny pieces of stone of different colors and sometimes glass to depict scenes of everyday life. Many that still survive show gladiators engaged in fighting.

GERMANIA

SARMATIA

DACIA

Pontus Euxinus

DALMATIA

ARMENIA

THRACIA

BITHYNIA

ITALIA

Roma

MACEDONIA

ASIA

EPIRUS

CILICIA

SYRIA

Sardinia

ACHAEA

Sicilia

Creta

Mare Internum

ARABIA

CYRENAICA

AEGYPTUS

The Roman Empire in AD 117

The Romans used war to expand their empire. Eventually the empire spread across Europe into parts of western Asia and northern Africa.

The Gladiatorial Games

The gladiatorial games quickly became the most popular form of entertainment in Rome. Originally, games were organized as a form of celebration at important funerals. It was believed that the killing of a gladiator would keep away evil spirits and please the gods. As a result, officials began preparing and planning their own funerals to involve bigger and more spectacular gladiatorial fights. Emperors, senators, and other powerful officials realized that holding gladiatorial games for pure entertainment would help them stay popular and in power.

MAXIMUS

Ridley Scott used the gladiators of Rome as the source for his 2000 film *Gladiator*, which starred Russell Crowe as the fallen General Maximus. Crowe worked so hard at becoming a gladiator that he broke bones in his foot and hip and injured both arms.

Games in action

It was common for many pairs of gladiators to fight in the arena at once. The largest games ever held involved 5,000 pairs of gladiators and were put on by Emperor Trajan in AD 107. The emperor sat with a group of senators in his box during the fight. Citizens sat in the stands.

Gladiatorial Time Line

The gladiatorial games began in 264 BC and were abolished 668 years later by Emperor Honorius in AD 404. As the popularity of the games grew, so did the number of people who became free gladiators. These were volunteers who elected to train and fight in the arena. They were not slaves. These volunteers were often poor men who fought in the hope of winning money.

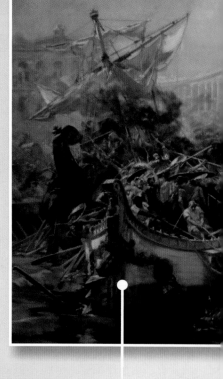

264 BC
The first recorded games are held in Rome, at the funeral of aristocrat Junius Brutus Pera.

202 BC
Wild animals are first used in gladiatorial games. Exotic animals are even brought from outside the empire.

80 BC
An amphitheater used for the games is built in Pompeii. It is later buried by the eruption of Mount Vesuvius.

46 BC
Julius Caesar builds an artificial lake and holds the first mock sea battle. It involves 3,000 gladiators.

AD 59
Nero is the firs to attempt to games. He bar for 10 years af among the spe

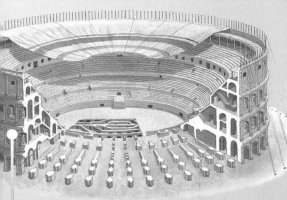

AD 70
ork begins on what will be
he most spectacular amphitheater
Roman history. In AD 83, Emperor Titus
pens the Colosseum. It has taken more
han 10 years to complete.

AD 200
Emperor Severus
bans female
gladiators from
competing in
the games.

AD 325
Emperor Constantine
bans the practice
of condemning
criminals to
gladiator schools.

AD 404
The gladiatorial
games are finally
abolished during
the reign of
Emperor Honorius.

Training to Be a Gladiator

S laves, prisoners, criminals, and free volunteers trained to be gladiators in gladiator schools. At the height of the games' popularity, there were up to 100 schools across the empire. The most famous of these were in Italy. They included Capua, which was near Naples, and the gladiator barracks in Pompeii. The most important school in Rome was the Ludus Magnus. This school was connected to the Colosseum by a tunnel.

Under the Colosseum
The area under the floor of the Colosseum held cells for men and cages for wild animals. The fighters were taken there, often from the Ludus Magnus, and locked up before a fight.

1 Gladiator cells
Gladiators were kept in cells and fed oatmeal, grains, beans, and barley. It was thought this diet would stop them from bleeding to death.

2 Cages connected to the arena
Before a fight, gladiators were kept in cages while they waited to be released into the arena.

Sacramentum gladiatorium
Each gladiator took an oath, agreeing to be treated as a slave without any rights. The oath was made to the gods.

"I WILL ENDURE TO BE BURNED, TO BE BOUND, TO BE BEATEN, AND TO BE KILLED BY THE SWORD."

URI · VINCIRI · VERBERARI FERROQUE NECARI

Remains of Pompeii barracks
The Pompeii gladiator barracks were situated behind the large theater. The remains of the barracks and cells can still be seen.

Training
Gladiators trained in the same groups each day and learned a set of routines. They were even trained in how to die in a way that looked graceful and pleased the crowd.

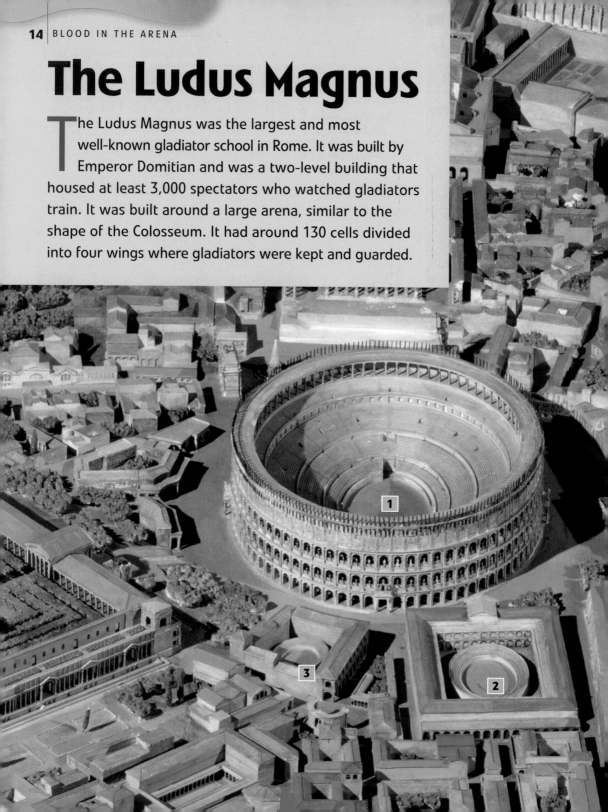

The Ludus Magnus

The Ludus Magnus was the largest and most well-known gladiator school in Rome. It was built by Emperor Domitian and was a two-level building that housed at least 3,000 spectators who watched gladiators train. It was built around a large arena, similar to the shape of the Colosseum. It had around 130 cells divided into four wings where gladiators were kept and guarded.

The Ludus Magnus today
The ruins of the Ludus Magnus today show half of the cells where gladiators were held.

THE TUNNEL

The Ludus Magnus closed when the games were abolished in AD 404. Its ruins were discovered in 1937 and a ground plan of the school was found in the Forum by archaeologists. It shows the underground tunnel connecting it to the Colosseum. The ground plan was part of a large marble plan of ancient Rome.

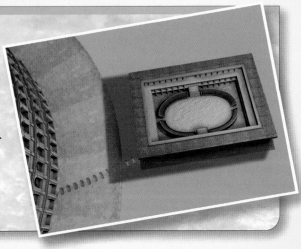

1 The Colosseum was the largest and most famous gladiator arena in all of the Roman Empire. The emperor hosted his own games there.

2 The Ludus Magnus was connected to the Colosseum by an underground tunnel. Gladiators were transported to the arena through this tunnel.

3 It is thought that the Ludus Matutinus was for training gladiators who fought animals. The name means "games of the morning," and battles against beasts were held in the morning.

Battle scenes
A mosaic near Rome shows gladiators fighting.
It was created in AD 320 and discovered in 1834.

Types of Gladiators

Gladiators were trained in various types of combat. This meant they used different kinds of weapons and armor, and they fought in different ways. Certain kinds of gladiators were often matched with particular types of opponents. Roman spectators most enjoyed seeing the Retiarii gladiators fight against the Secutores, while Murmillones, Thraeces, and Hoplomachi usually fought each other.

Bestiarii
These often carried a swor
and shield and fought larg
wild animals, such as tiger

ssedarii

ese drove chariots and
rried a sword for hand
mbat. They may have
ught wild animals.

Secutores

These had smooth helmets
so they did not get caught in
Retiarii nets. They carried a
shield and sword.

Retiarii

These fought with a trident
as their main weapon. They
carried a net to trap their
opponents.

loplomachi

ased on the Spartan
plite, these carried a
rge, rounded shield and
ay have had full body
rmor and a sword.

Andabatae

These wore helmets
with no eyeholes. They
rode on horseback and
charged with swords.

Dimachaeri

These were renowned for
wearing no protective
armor. They fought with
two daggers and no shield.

Types of Weapons and Armor

Weapons and armor became more important as the popularity of the games increased. At the height of the games, there were many different types of weaponry and armor, all designed for a specific fighting style. These included swords and bows, helmets and breastplates, and different kinds of shields. Armor was made of various metals or leather. Metal offered more protection but was heavier to wear. Leather was lighter and allowed better movement but could be more easily pierced with a weapon.

Scutum
Designed to protect the body, this shield was rectangular or oval in shape.

Pilum
Similar to a javelin, this long pole had a sharp metal point.

Rete
This net was made from strong rope. Usually it had weights, and sometimes blades, attached to its ends.

Laquesus missilis
This was a lasso made from strong leather or rope and was similar to the rete.

Cataphracts
These fabric tunics had bits of leather or metal sewn into them for added protection.

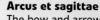
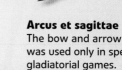

Arcus et sagittae
The bow and arrow was used only in special gladiatorial games.

1 Helmet
Helmets were made from both metal and leather.

2 Manica
The manica was a piece of leather armor worn on the arm.

3 Breastplate
Breastplates were made of bronze and protected the whole torso.

4 Acinaces
This straight, single-edged sword was a common weapon.

Dressed for battle
Strong, well-made armor and weapons were the difference between life and death in the arena.

5 Parmula
This small defensive shield was round or oval.

6 Trident
The trident was a long spear with three prongs on the end.

Spartacus

Spartacus left his home in Greece to join the Roman army. He later deserted, was captured, and was sold into slavery. As a slave he was sent to gladiator school in Capua. In 73 BC, Spartacus the gladiator led a revolt for freedom. The 70–80 slaves gathered escaped with weapons and set up camp on Mount Vesuvius, where more rebel slaves later joined them. The Roman senate sent a legion of 3,000 soldiers to end the revolt. Spartacus and his men defeated them. The senate sent two more legions that were also defeated. Spartacus died in battle in 71 BC.

Statue of honor
Spartacus was a Thracian gladiator. He wore a broad helmet and carried a curved sword.

FLAMMA

Flamma was one of the most popular gladiators of all time. He was a soldier in Syria who was condemned to be a gladiator for insubordination. A gladiator could earn his freedom after winning five fights or surviving several years of battle. Flamma was awarded his freedom four times but chose to stay a gladiator. Flamma was so popular that his head appeared on a Roman coin.

The inscription on Flamma's gravestone

FLAMMA
"LOACH"

SECUTOR GLADIATOR

LIVED TO 30 YEARS OLD

FOUGHT 34 TIMES

WON 21 TIMES

DREW 9 TIMES

DEFEATED 4 TIMES

Brave and bold
Before the final battle, Spartacus killed his own horse as a symbol of his determination.

Death of aide
Spartacus's chief aide, Crixus, was killed during the second conflict with the Roman soldiers. To avenge his aide's death, Spartacus forced 300 prisoners from that conflict to battle in pairs to the death, as gladiators did.

Circus Maximus

The first and largest stadium to be built in ancient Rome, this racetrack hosted many events, such as gladiator matches, boxing, foot races, and chariot races. The Circus Maximus was originally built from wood and destroyed by fire in 31 BC. After two more fires, a new marble stadium was built in AD 103. The two sides of the oval-shaped racing track were divided by a raised median called a *spina*. There was a turning post at one end of the spina called a *meta*.

Circus Maximus today
All that remains today is the now grass-covered track, the *spina*, and some starting ga

Chariot racing

Chariot racing was the most popular event at the Circus, with up to 12 races a day. Chariots were small and designed to be as lightweight as possible. They were usually drawn by two or four horses.

Circus Maximus as it was

The arena was more than 2,000 feet (600 m) long and 387 feet (118 m) wide. The stadium seated 150,000 spectators and was three stories high.

The Colosseum

The Colosseum was the largest amphitheater of its time. Building began in AD 70, and it took 20,000–30,000 slaves and skilled workers more than 10 years to finish. To celebrate, Emperor Titus held a 100-day festival of games. This included spectacular gladiator and animal shows. The amphitheater was four stories high and measured 617 feet (188 m) by 512 feet (156 m).

Emperor's
The emperor sat in
Imperial Box. The box
located on the podiu
the north side of the ar
A tunnel connected
Imperial Box to the Imp
Palace. The senators also
at this le

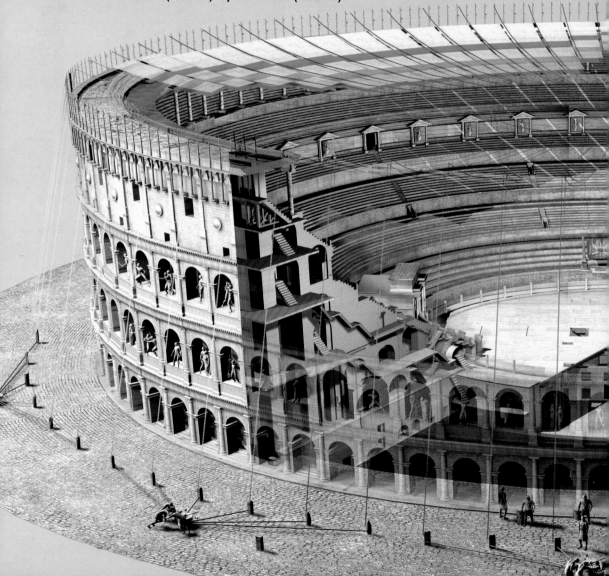

Entrances
The Colosseum had 76 entrance gate arches that the general public used. There were also four grand entrance gate arches that were used only by the emperors, officials, and wealthy Romans.

Upper-level seats
The upper-level seats were for women and the lower social classes. They were steep wooden seats.

Lower-level seats
The first tier of marble seats was used by the nobles. The second tier of marble seats was reserved for wealthy citizens.

Sail-cloth awning
The velarium, or awning, provided shade for spectators. It covered one-third of the arena and sloped down toward the center. The awning was held up by long ropes that passed down to street level where they were controlled by winches.

Colosseum construction

The Colosseum was built from marble, concrete, brick, and stone. Although it was damaged by fire and an earthquake, much of it has lasted for thousands of years.

Emperor Gladiators

A small number of emperors, wanting popularity and to establish a reputation for bravery, entered the arena as gladiators. Although gladiators were considered the lowest of the social classes, exceptional gladiators won fame and respect from their spectators. There were some emperors who sought this same kind of fame. However, unlike real gladiators, emperors were safe in battle because these contests were fixed and staged. Emperors chose their opponents and set the rules of the fight.

CALIGULA

Emperor Caligula was considered a very cruel emperor gladiator. He used the games to show his power and authority. He demanded that ordinary citizens, not trained gladiators, fight him in the arena. One account states that he killed his opponent by producing a real sword in a wooden sword battle. He also removed the awning in the Colosseum on hot days so that he could watch the crowd suffer. When he first became emperor, Caligula had a temporary pontoon bridge built over a bay and—dressed as a Thracian gladiator—rode over it on horseback.

Gladiator for sale
In his court in Rome, Emperor Caligula selected gladiator slaves to purchase.

COMMODUS

Emperor Commodus was known for his vanity in the arena. He would dress as Hercules and battle wild animals, specifically lions. In one case it is said that he slaughtered 100 bears. Commodus also charged the people large amounts of money to see his fights. This eventually damaged Rome's economy. Just as Caligula had done, Commodus fought against ordinary citizens in the arena.

The Decline of the Games

Historians give two main reasons for the decline of the games: the failing Roman economy and the growth of Christianity. The games were extremely expensive to put on. As Rome's economy began to struggle during the period AD 300–400, it became harder to hold such elaborate entertainment. With the rise of Christianity, the number of people who saw the games as cruel increased and they began to protest against them. Emperor Constantine gave Christians the freedom to worship in AD 313, and Honorius closed all gladiator schools in AD 399. The games were abolished completely in AD 404 when a spectator trying to stop a fight was killed.

" . . . I chanced to drop in a the midday games, expectin sport . . . and some relaxati to rest men's eyes from th sight of human blood. Just t opposite was the case . . it was plain butchery."

Philosopher's influence
After attending the games, the Roman philosopher Seneca was upset that crowds watched gladiators being killed for pleasure

Did You Know?
Women too fought as gladiators. Some were slaves but others were wealthy women who possibly did it for excitement. Emperor Severus banned female gladiators in AD 200.

The teachings of Jesus
Christians believed the games went against the teachings of Christ. But some Christian emperors continued to support the games.

Protest
Spectators would sometimes enter the arena to try and stop a gladiatorial fight. According to legend, the monk Telemachus was stoned to death when he tried to stop a fight.

Be a Roman Gladiator!

Imagine that you are a Roman gladiator. Keep a journal and write an entry for each day in one week in your life. Refer to this book to make your entries as authentic as possible. You might also like to add pictures and captions.

Here are some questions to help you with your writing:

1 What type of gladiator will you be?

2 What kinds of weapons and armor will you have?

3 Where will you do your training?

4 Where will you fight and why?

5 What will your living quarters be like?

6 How will a day in your life be spent?

7 What is your family background?

8 How many fights have you fought already?

Glossary

arena (uh-REE-nuh) A level area that is surrounded by seats for spectactors.

aristocrat (uh-RIS-tuh-krat) A person belonging to the higher levels of a society.

citizens (SIH-tih-zenz) Legally recognized members of a state, nationality, or country.

economy (ih-KAH-nuh-mee) The wealth and resources of a society.

Forum (FOR-um) A popular meeting place in the center of Rome.

legion (LEE-jen) A unit of 3,000–6,000 men in the Roman army.

opponent (uh-POH-nent) A person or a group that is against another.

podium (POH-dee-um) A platform on which a person stands so that they can be seen by the audience.

pontoon (pahn-TOON) A flat-bottomed boat or hollow metal cylinders used to support a temporary or floating bridge.

revolt (rih-VOLT) An uprising or rebellion by a group of people.

senators (SEH-nuh-terz) Members of ancient Rome's senate.

tradition (truh-DIH-shun) A way of doing something that has been passed down over time.

Index

Websites

Due to the changing nature of Internet links, PowerKids Press has developed an online list of websites related to the subject of this book. This site is updated regularly. Please use this link to access the list: www.powerkidslinks.com/disc/glad/